MEANT FOR GOOD

THE ADVENTURE OF TRUSTING GOD & HIS PLANS FOR YOU

SIX-SESSION STUDY GUIDE

BY MEGAN FATE MARSHMAN

HarperChristian Resources

Meant for Good Study Guide
© 2020 by Megan Fate Marshman

Requests for information should be addressed to:
HarperChristian Resources, 3900 Sparks Dr. SE, Grand Rapids, MI 49546

ISBN 978-0-310-11380-5 (softcover)
ISBN 978-0-310-11381-2 (ebook)

All Scripture quotations, unless otherwise indicated, are taken from The Holy Bible, New International Version®, NIV®. Copyright © 1973, 1978, 1984, 2011 by Biblica, Inc.® Used by permission of Zondervan. All rights reserved worldwide.www.Zondervan.com. The "NIV" and "New International Version" are trademarks registered in the United States Patent and Trademark Office by Biblica, Inc.®

Any internet addresses (websites, blogs, etc.) and telephone numbers in this study guide are offered as a resource. They are not intended in any way to be or imply an endorsement by HarperChristian Resources, nor does HarperChristian Resources vouch for the content of these sites and numbers for the life of this study guide.

HarperChristian Resources titles may be purchased in bulk for church, business, fundraising, or ministry use. For information, please e-mail ResourceSpecialist@ChurchSource.com.

Cover design: Brand Navigation
Interior design: CrosslinCreative.net

First Printing June 2020 / Printed in the United States of America

CONTENTS

THE GOSPEL

In the beginning, God created everything. He created humanity to share and enjoy His love. But something went wrong.

Although humankind had a beautiful, intimate relationship with God, humanity chose to rebel—something we still choose to do to this day. They broke their relationship with God and earned a consequence called "death." Death simply means separation. When they sinned, their spirits died—they were separated from God. It wasn't just them. We *all* have one thing in common: we all fall short and need a savior (Romans 3:23).

The only one who lives up to God's perfect standard is *God, so God* sent Himself. Jesus—fully God and fully man—came to earth and lived a perfect life, thereby earning a perfect relationship with His heavenly Father. We earned separation, but He didn't give us what we earned because of His love. The love He *demonstrated* by dying on the cross for us (Romans 5:8).

Why did Jesus have to die? If He didn't, our "falling short" would've resulted in us being forever separated from God, even after death. The consequence for our sin is death, but the gift of God is eternal life through Jesus (Romans 6:23). One day, we'll all die physically. But this also refers to spiritual death. We deserve eternal separation from God.

But . . . the story doesn't end there. God doesn't force us to pay the ultimate debt of our life. He pays it Himself with the sacrifice and gift of Jesus' life.

Why did Jesus have to die? His death is in place of *our* death. Our consequence for falling short was put on Him, and He was killed in our place. But the gift keeps giving. Jesus rose from the grave and defeated death and lives forever at God's side. *Now*, you and I can receive the gift of a restored perfect relationship with God. We earned separation from God, *but* Jesus offers us forever life with Him instead. We are not capable of overcoming death, but death is the only payment to bring restoration to our relationship with God. Jesus paid the price and overcame the consequence on our behalf. All we must do is acknowledge we are sinners, surrender our lives to His lordship, and believe that God raised Him from the dead (Romans 10:9). Then we can be forgiven for our sins, receive His gracious gift, and step into the restored life Jesus offers. Everything in this study is built on this amazing gospel truth.

NOTE FROM
THE AUTHOR

I don't like being disappointed.

Every disappointment, trivial or tragic, is the result of unmet expectations. Therefore, our expectations as we approach this study matter.

Here are my expectations: I want the you who finishes this study to be different than the you who started it. I want you to go beyond what you know and feel and start seeing what God has in store for you, and trust Him with all you've got. The difference between head-knowledge and the real depth of what God has for us is the difference between a mud puddle and the Pacific Ocean. It's huge.

In large part, we'll be studying Jeremiah 29:11—14. While everyone loves Jeremiah 29:11, we will be reminded why the chapter doesn't end there. There's so much more to unpack in the verses after verse 11—truth you need in your life today! How do I know? Because I have needed these truths in my own life.

I run into people all the time who disclose to me, "I'm just *trying* to trust God right now," and I wonder if they know what it practically looks like to trust Him. Our definition of "trust" can be a bit cloudy. Are they trusting, or are they hanging onto the hope that their life is going to work out the way they want it to? That's not trust—that's just a bunch of expectations ready to be unmet. That's an exercise in being disappointed, not in trusting God.

Lucky for us, Jeremiah wrote verses 12-14 to teach the Israelites precisely *how* to trust God. Does actively and consistently trusting God sound overwhelming? Let me simplify. If you want to draw closer to God, you're in the right place. If you're here to seek God, you won't be disappointed with what you find. Not because of my words on these pages, but because God promises you'll find Him if you do (Jeremiah 29:13). And once you find Him, you'll have everything you need.

Megan Fate Marshman

WHAT'S THIS STUDY ALL ABOUT?

Spiritual growth is the way God forms us more into the likeness of His Son, Jesus. This study is all about God's plans to reach the world, your neighborhood, and even your family. And, guess what? His plans involve you. The process of discovering your part in God's plans require a Christ-centered community and a submission to His Spirit as He forms you more into the likeness of Jesus. This process is not gathering information, it's submitting your plans for His. As you discover what God is doing in you and learn to say "Yes!" to His leading, you'll be empowered to live the life of purpose you were created for. Get ready for an adventure. God's plans are meant for good . . . and His good plans involve you.

GATHER (GROUP STUDY)

The group gatherings are intended to be 90 minutes of connection with each other and God.

> ### PREPARE!
> This section has a few quick activities to help you check in with yourself **before** you show up to your gathering. Do it any time the day of or in the car outside of your gathering.

> ### HEAR FROM MEGAN—VIDEO
> Each session is kicked off with a video teaching from Megan. Follow the video outline and take notes if you like.

> ### GROUP DISCUSSION
> The greatest growth is found in group discussion where we share our experiences, perspectives, questions, and encouragement. There will be prompts to read and corresponding questions to explore each session's teaching further.

STUDY & SEEK (PERSONAL STUDY)

Study & Seek is the personal study component of the *Meant for Good* Study Guide. These exercises are designed to take you into relevant Scripture where you can grow with God's leading in specific and personal ways. Go at your own pace doing a little each day or do it all at once.

▶ *WALK IN STEP*

These personal study exercises will have you engage with a passage of Scripture and commentary taking Megan's teaching one step deeper. Each exercise is intentional and encourages willingness to experience change and growth—the goal is always to become more like Jesus and to trust God's plan more completely.

▶ *LIVE LIKE CHRIST*

Discover action steps to help you apply what God has been doing in your heart to your everyday life.

LEADER'S NOTE:

Make sure you check out the Leader's Guide in the back of this book to help you prepare for each group gathering.

Encourage your partipants to make use of the blank pages for notes in the back of this guide.

GOD'S PLANS ARE MEANT FOR GOOD

GATHER

Group Study

PREPARE!

Before you show up to your gathering, check in with yourself.

① THE TITLE OF TODAY IS: _____

Title your day as if it were a chapter title in the book of your life. Be creative and not hasty. Think about the entire day or week you've had, not just the past hour.

② YOUR MOOD: Circle all that apply.

③ ENERGY LEVEL: Mark along the line.

Blah . . .   Let's Do This!

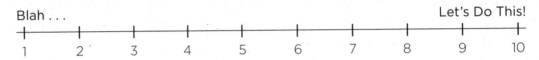

1   2   3   4   5   6   7   8   9   10

④ I AM THANKFUL FOR:

_____

_____

_____

⑤ MY HEART FEELS HEAVY BECAUSE:

_____

_____

_____

① MY ONE-WORD PRAYER FOR TODAY: _____

Write out one word or sentence that could encapsulate a lot of what you are hoping to hear or discover today with God's help.

"TELL ME, WHAT
IS IT YOU **PLAN** TO
DO WITH YOUR
ONE WILD AND
PRECIOUS LIFE."

—MARY OLIVER

GATHERING TRANSITION TIME (10 minutes)

> **RELEVANT VERSES:**
> ### JEREMIAH 29:11-14
> ### ROMANS 8:28-29

WHO ARE YOU & WHY ARE YOU HERE?

Take 3 minutes to fill in the following questions.

Name: _____

1. Where did you grow up? _____

2. What is your go-to karaoke song? _____

3. What is your favorite room in your home? _____

4. What is the most impactful book you've read lately? _____

Using only three words, answer this:
Why are you here today?

_____   _____   _____

Go around the room taking turns introducing yourself and sharing your
3 words to the group before you begin the teaching video.

SESSION 1 VIDEO (17 minutes)

Let's watch the video for this session and feel free to take notes below.

> **NOTES:**
> God can and will be found when you search for Him with all
> your heart.

Everything God does is meant for good

God defines good differently than we define good.

God's good plans are not exempt from trial.

Rather than saving you from trials, God wants to transform you *through* them.

Your past will either be Satan's weapon against you or God's most powerful tool.

WHAT'S GOD SAYING? (3 Minutes)

Take a minute on your own to look over your notes and write down what stands out, resonates, or challenges you most. Then have one or two people briefly share.

_____

_____

_____

"TO **WALK OUT**
OF HIS WILL IS
TO WALK INTO
NOWHERE."

—C.S. LEWIS

THINK BEFORE YOU SPEAK
(5 Minutes)

Pick one person to read aloud to the group before you begin group discussion.

UNDERSTANDING ROMANS

When the Apostle Paul wrote the letter to the church in Rome, trust in Jesus was sweeping across the Roman Empire, but with that trust came heavy oppression (and at times even death). So, it would have been pretty surprising for Paul to write that God is working out *all* things for the good. What good could possibly come out of these awful circumstances??

Paul is encouraging those trusting in Jesus to have a different perspective and approach to life, no matter how difficult life can be. This is why in the next verse, Paul tells us what he means by "good": "For those God foreknew he also predestined to be conformed to the image of his Son, that he might be the firstborn among many brothers and sisters" (Romans 8:29). God's good plan for us is to form us more into the likeness of Jesus. The "good" God has for you is to transform you into the image of His Son so that you can partner with Him in the restoration of all things. His plans for our lives are so much bigger and better than ours.

In our **GROUP DISCUSSION**, we are going to explore four approaches to trusting God's good plan.

_____

_____

_____

_____

GROUP DISCUSSION (30-40 Min

Leader, read each numbered prompt out loud and ask the correspond
discussion question.

WE KNOW GOD WORKS

And we know that in all things God works for the good of those who love him, who have been called according to his purpose. For those God foreknew he also predestined to be conformed to the image of his Son, that he might be the firstborn among many brothers and sisters. —Romans 8:28-29

- How is Paul's definition of "good" in Romans 8:29 (to be conformed to the image of his Son) different than the cultural definition of good?

2 ALL THINGS FOR GOOD

God can use "all things" to further His good plans. He can use "all things" to conform us more into the image of His Son so we can partner with Him in the restoration of all things. God's plans for our lives are so much bigger and better than ours.

- As you consider God using "all things" in your life for good, which part of your life comes to mind?

- What part of your life might God be wanting to use for good?

GOD'S PLANS ARE MEANT FOR GOOD

TO BE CONFORMED

Spiritual formation is the process by which Christ is formed in us. It's not solely about gathering information although information is part of the necessary fertilizer that allows spiritual formation to take root. Spiritual formation is also not defined by what we do or don't do. Rather, it depends upon what *Christ is doing in us*. To be conformed to the image of Christ, we must discover truth *and* be willing to submit our plans to God's plans. The appropriate response is not gripping harder and trying to control areas of our lives, it's opening up our hands in submission.

- How might Jesus be inviting you to open your hands and submit control of an area of your life to Him?

- How specifically might Jesus be inviting you to open your hands and submit control to Him?

" . . . BE CONFORMED TO THE IMAGE OF HIS SON . . ."

4

TO THE IMAGE OF HIS SON

God can use all things "to conform us to the image of His Son." He can use our talents, our roles, our relationships, and even our trials for His glory and our good. God doesn't remove us *from* trials, He transforms us *through* them. "All things" can be meant for good.

- How might God be wanting to use the very things you're going through to conform you more into the likeness of Jesus?

- What could be your next best step?

- And how can we help?

RECEIVE BLESSING
(5 Minutes)

Leader, have everyone sit with hands open, palms up. Read the following blessing over your group before closing in prayer.

> May you find all confidence in God's plan and promise to make you more like Christ.

CLOSING PRAYER (5 Minutes)

Encourage the group to engage the personal study material throughout the week before your next gathering. Pray in whichever way best suits your group, and use this space to keep track of prayer requests and praises. Dismiss!

GOD'S **PLANS** ARE MEANT FOR GOOD

STUDY AND SEEK

Personal Study

WALK IN STEP

THE MAIN CHARACTER

When studying scripture, it is important to recognize we are not the main character, God is. First and foremost, the Bible is the story of a radically loving God chasing tirelessly after those He created. So, as you approach these **Walk in Step** sections, look for what they reveal about who He is first. This will help you in joining Him where He is going, rather than trying to get Him to help *you* with where *you* want to go.

Read the following passage three times:

MARK 4:35-41

> 35 That day when evening came, he said to his disciples, "Let us go over to the other side." 36 Leaving the crowd behind, they took him along, just as he was, in the boat. There were also other boats with him. 37 A furious squall came up, and the waves broke over the boat, so that it was nearly swamped. 38 Jesus was in the stern, sleeping on a cushion. The disciples woke him and said to him, "Teacher, don't you care if we drown?"

> 39 He got up, rebuked the wind and said to the waves, "Quiet! Be still!" Then the wind died down and it was completely calm.

> 40 He said to his disciples, "Why are you so afraid? Do you still have no faith?"

> 41 They were terrified and asked each other, "Who is this? Even the wind and the waves obey him!"

Next, write down 30 OBSERVATIONS about the passage and what you notice in the chart.

30 OBSERVATIONS

1. _____
2. _____
3. _____
4. _____
5. _____

So far so good!

6. _____
7. _____
8. _____
9. _____
10. _____

Now you're rolling!

11. _____
12. _____
13. _____
14. _____
15. _____

Half way there!

16. _____
17. _____
18. _____
19. _____
20. _____

Crushing it!

21. _____
22. _____
23. _____
24. _____
25. _____

You go this!

26. _____
27. _____
28. _____
29. _____
30. _____

Told you it was possible!

Circle the three most significant observations to you. Based on your observations, write what you think God is saying to you through this passage in a single line:

_____

▶ MINDFULNESS

God meets us precisely where we are. It's important we approach His truth being honest about where we are. Spend a few minutes becoming mindful of your body, mind, and spirit.

As you become aware of each part of your body, slowly shade in the outline. Further darken the areas of pain, soreness, discomfort, or exhaustion.

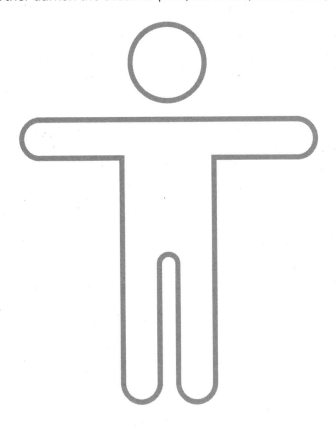

What three things are weighing heaviest on your mind today? Write them here.

1. _____

2. _____

3. _____

▶ TRUTH IS . . .

Read the truth statements below and circle the **3** that feel most difficult to fully believe right now.

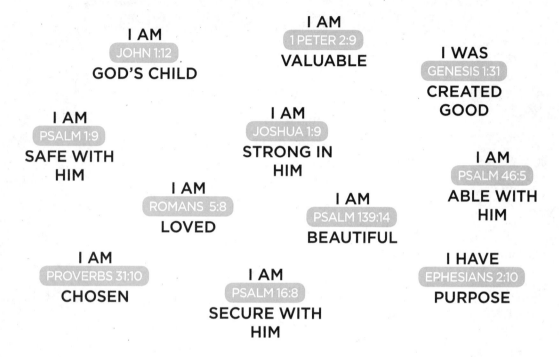

I AM
JOHN 1:12
GOD'S CHILD

I AM
1 PETER 2:9
VALUABLE

I WAS
GENESIS 1:31
CREATED GOOD

I AM
PSALM 1:9
SAFE WITH HIM

I AM
JOSHUA 1:9
STRONG IN HIM

I AM
ROMANS 5:8
LOVED

I AM
PSALM 139:14
BEAUTIFUL

I AM
PSALM 46:5
ABLE WITH HIM

I AM
PROVERBS 31:10
CHOSEN

I AM
PSALM 16:8
SECURE WITH HIM

I HAVE
EPHESIANS 2:10
PURPOSE

Look up the verse associated to each of the three truths most difficult to believe right now. Write out each verse and as you do, invite God to help you fully trust Him at His word.

TRUTH 1:

TRUTH 2:

TRUTH 3:

PSALM 23

The Lord is my shepherd, I lack nothing.
    He makes me lie down in green pastures,
he leads me beside quiet waters,
    he refreshes my soul.
He guides me along the right paths
    for his name's sake.
Even though I walk
    through the darkest valley,
I will fear no evil,
    for you are with me;
your rod and your staff,
    they comfort me.

You prepare a table before me
    in the presence of my enemies.
You anoint my head with oil;
    my cup overflows.
Surely your goodness and love will follow me
    all the days of my life,
and I will dwell in the house of the Lord
    forever.

HOW DO YOU NEED GOD TO BE YOUR SHEPHERD TODAY?

Notice, Psalm 23 is more about Who God is than who we are. Using the guided outline below, write out your own personal psalm acknowledging who God is, what He does, and how you plan to trust Him precisely where you're at in response.

The LORD is _____

He _____

_____

He _____

_____

He _____

_____

Even though I _____

_____

I will _____

_____

for you are _____

_____

You have _____

_____

You have _____

Surely your goodness and love will follow me all the days of my life,

and I will dwell in the house of the LORD forever.

LIVE LIKE CHRIST

PIE CHART:

Create a pie chart in the heart below based on what is consuming the most space in your heart. Label each piece of your chart to better see what you are trusting in right now.

> *Some areas of trust may be yourself, a job/career, wealth, romantic relationship, friends, health, fitness, education, intelligence, accomplishments, etc.*

ACTION STEPS

Based on your chart, write down three action steps you want to pursue in the next week that you believe will help shift the focus of your heart more toward God.

ACTION STEP 1:

ACTION STEP 2:

ACTION STEP 3:

SESSION

WE ARE
INVITED
TO TRUST

GATHER

Group Study

PREPARE!

Before you show up to your gathering, check in with yourself.

① THE TITLE OF TODAY IS: _____

Title your day as if it were a chapter title in the book of your life. Be creative and not hasty. Think about the entire day or week you've had, not just the past hour.

② YOUR MOOD: Circle all that apply.

③ ENERGY LEVEL: Mark along the line.

Blah . . .   Let's Do This!

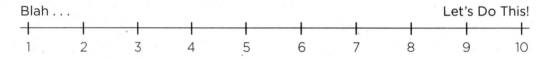

1   2   3   4   5   6   7   8   9   10

④ I AM THANKFUL FOR:

_____

_____

_____

⑤ MY HEART FEELS HEAVY BECAUSE:

_____

_____

_____

① MY ONE-WORD PRAYER FOR TODAY: _____

Write out one word or sentence that could encapsulate a lot of what you are hoping to hear or discover today with God's help.

"NEVER BE AFRAID TO **TRUST** AN UNKNOWN FUTURE TO A KNOWN GOD."

—CORRIE TEN BOOM

GATHERING TRANSITION TIME (10 minutes)

> ### *RELEVANT VERSES:*
> ## **GENESIS** 1
> ## **GENESIS** 3:9

Using only three words, write the answer to the following question and share with your group:

How would you describe your personal Study & Seek *time learning precisely where your heart is as you began to dig in this week?*

_____ _____ _____

> *Share one or two action steps you wrote down in your STUDY & SEEK time. Allow your group to join you in living out these steps as your accountability partners.*

SESSION 2 **VIDEO** (20 minutes)

Let's watch the video for this session and feel free to take notes below.

> ### *NOTES:*
> God is the main character of the story.

Shame leads us to hide, blame, shame, fear, and anxiety.

God pursues us in the midst of our guilt and shame.

God frees us then shows us how to live like we are free.

God came down the ladder to us.

Listening is an act of trust.

THE GOSPEL (5 Minutes)

▸ **Before we begin** our group discussion on the video teaching, it is important for us to all get on the same page when it comes to the Gospel. For some of us the "Good News" is a new and exciting concept. Others of us have a version of the Gospel in our heads—even if it is somewhat vague—presented to us by a family member or friend, in Sunday school, or at Christian camp. No matter where each of us is at, it is good for us to level the playing field and acknowledge this very same story applies to every single one of us in the very same way. Turn to the beginning of your study guide (page iv) and have one person read the Gospel to the group.

WHAT'S GOD SAYING? (5 Minutes)

Take a minute on your own to consider and write down what stands out, resonates, or challenges you most about the video and what you just read about the Gospel. Then we'll have one or two people briefly share.

_____

_____

_____

_____

_____

_____

"**LISTENING** IS
NOT WAITING
FOR YOUR TURN
TO TALK."

—MEGAN

"BEFORE YOU SPEAK IT IS NECESSARY FOR YOU TO **LISTEN**, FOR GOD SPEAKS IN THE **SILENCE** OF THE HEART."

—MOTHER TERESA

THINK BEFORE YOU SPEAK
(5 Minutes)

Pick one person to read aloud to the group before you begin group discussion.

UNDERSTANDING SHAME

In Genesis 2:25 we read, "Adam and his wife were both naked, and they felt no shame." Yes they were physically naked, but the Hebrew poetry found in the creation story is pointing to a deeper nakedness, to be fully known with no desire to hide. Imagine that for a second, trusting someone so much you show and offer them all of yourself. Humanity felt no shame in front of each other and no shame before their Creator. This is this kind of intimacy Jesus has come to restore. An intimacy between us and God *and* us and each other. When disobedience enters the picture in Genesis 3, sin sends humanity into a cycle of shame, causing us to hide from each other and God. It is only through Jesus' grace-filled pursuit that this isolating cycle can be overcome. He opens the door for us to again hear God's voice and be lifted into the cycle of trust we were always designed for. A cycle we will explore more in depth on the next page.

In our **GROUP DISCUSSION**, we are going to look at Genesis 3:6-8 and explore together how the cycle of trust is hijacked by a cycle of shame.

_____

_____

_____

_____

_____

GROUP DISCUSSION (30-40 Minutes)

Leader, read each numbered prompt out loud and ask the corresponding discussion question.

1

GENESIS 3:6-8

When the woman saw that the fruit of the tree was good for food and pleasing to the eye, and also desirable for gaining wisdom, she took some and ate it. She also gave some to her husband, who was with her, and he ate it. Then the eyes of both of them were opened, and they realized they were naked; so they sewed fig leaves together and made coverings for themselves.

Then the man and his wife heard the sound of the Lord God as he was walking in the garden in the cool of the day, and they hid from the Lord God among the trees of the garden.

- What might Jesus be trying to say to us in this passage?
- Discuss the connection between the passage and the graphic. In what ways has your trust or lack of trust affected your ability to hear God's voice?

CONNECTION WITH **GOD**

CYCLE OF **Trust**

LOVE & OBEDIENCE

TRUST RESPONSE

2

CYCLE OF TRUST

God knows we cannot get to Him on our own. That is why the *Cycle of Trust* always starts with God moving towards us. Through Jesus, He continuously and lovingly pursues His creation, speaking to each of our hearts softly, yet powerfully. Like a patient visitor, God's voice waits to be received and welcomed in. By receiving God's voice into our *Inner You*, we allow God's creative and transformative power to soak more and more into the innermost parts of us. When we allow our response to flow from God's restorative work in our hearts, His strength carries us into a loving and obedient response. Though this does not happen all at once (we tend to trust God a little at a time), through our continued reception and response of trust, He can carry us to greater connectedness with Himself and He can transform us to become more of who He created us to be.

- How have you noticed God's pursuit of you through His loving voice?
- What do you think keeps you from listening to His voice?

CYCLE OF SHAME

In our fallen world, we are being bombarded with lying voices at every turn. Like a thief, these voices hope to force their way into the *Inner You*. It takes an active heart *not* to receive them. When allowed, these voices stake their own claim in our hearts and can easily spiral us into a *Cycle of Shame*. These voices convince us that we are unacceptable in our nakedness, pushing us to respond through hiding and blame. These shame responses lead us into further isolation, as we choose to close God and others out, believing we can only trust in ourselves. This creates space for greater lies to reign in our hearts. The only way we can truly combat these lies is allowing God and His powerful voice of truth in.

- How have you seen lying voices push you or others into a Cycle of Shame?
- How can receiving God's voice into the Inner You help to combat this cycle?

GOD'S VOICE

LYING VOICES

THE INNER **YOU**

CYCLE OF **SHAME**

SHAME RESPONSE

HIDING & BLAME

ISOLATION FROM **GOD**

RECEIVE BLESSING
(5 Minutes)

Leader, have everyone sit with hands open, palms up. Read the following blessing over your group before closing in prayer.

May your heart be moved and changed by the truth you hear and may you always have ears to hear it.

CLOSING PRAYER (5 Minutes)

Encourage the group to engage the personal study material throughout the week before your next gathering. Pray in whichever way best suits your group, and use this space to keep track of prayer requests and praises. Dismiss!

WE ARE INVITED TO TRUST

STUDY AND SEEK

Personal Study

WALK IN STEP

RECOGNIZING GOD'S VOICE

Recognizing God's voice isn't something that comes without practice and intentionality. To learn the uniquely loving tone and truthful tambour, it will take time spent reading and familiarizing ourselves with God's written word, the Bible. It is also helpful to practice quieting our hearts from all other voices and distractions as we listen for Him alone. Even the great prophet Elijah allowed fear to drown out God's voice at times. Read about how God guides Him back.

Read the following passage three times:

- The first time, **underline** all the words and phrases that stand out to you.

- The second, **write** all the **questions** you have about the passage as they come up.

- The third time around, **circle** the **key words** or phrases God might be highlighting for you.

Afterward, rewrite the passage in your own words.

1 KINGS 19:3-13

³ Elijah was afraid and ran for his life. When he came to Beersheba in Judah, he left his servant there, ⁴ while he himself went a day's journey into the wilderness. He came to a broom bush, sat down under it and prayed that he might die. "I have had enough, Lord," he said. "Take my life; I am no better than my ancestors." ⁵ Then he lay down under the bush and fell asleep.

All at once an angel touched him and said, "Get up and eat." ⁶ He looked around, and there by his head was some bread baked over hot coals, and a jar of water. He ate and drank and then lay down again.

⁷ The angel of the Lord came back a second time and touched him and said, "Get up and eat, for the journey is too much for you." ⁸ So he got up and ate and drank. Strengthened by that food, he traveled forty days

and forty nights until he reached Horeb, the mountain of God. 9 There he went into a cave and spent the night.

And the word of the Lord came to him: "What are you doing here, Elijah?"

10 He replied, "I have been very zealous for the Lord God Almighty. The Israelites have rejected your covenant, torn down your altars, and put your prophets to death with the sword. I am the only one left, and now they are trying to kill me too."

11 The Lord said, "Go out and stand on the mountain in the presence of the Lord, for the Lord is about to pass by."

Then a great and powerful wind tore the mountains apart and shattered the rocks before the Lord, but the Lord was not in the wind. After the wind there was an earthquake, but the Lord was not in the earthquake. 12 After the earthquake came a fire, but the Lord was not in the fire. And after the fire came a gentle whisper. 13 When Elijah heard it, he pulled his cloak over his face and went out and stood at the mouth of the cave.

Then a voice said to him, "What are you doing here, Elijah?"

THE NEW (Your Name) _____ VERSION

Rewrite the passage in your own words below making a personal paraphrase.
Then answer the questions on the next page.

1 KINGS 19:3-13

> *A personal paraphrase (like Eugene Peterson's The Message Bible) is
> a rephrasing of an already translated passage into your own words.
> It does not mean your words are a valid translation, but it can be an
> eye opening exercise.*

_____

_____

_____

_____

_____

_____

_____

_____

_____

_____

_____

_____

_____

_____

_____

_____

1. Describe a time in your life during which exceptional trust in God was challenged or required. Was your response to trust God or yourself? How did it work out?

2. For all the truth you know of God and His character, what is the greatest obstacle you face trusting in Him completely?

3. Describe a time God called you out and you hid in shame. Imagine going through the same circumstance but with a deeper understanding of God's promise to love and embrace you. How would actively trusting God's promise have changed your response?

4. What do you need to change or embrace to be transformed by God's promise of love and live truly free right now?

▶ THE INNER ME

Use the letters on the left side of the page to make an acrostic describing how the Inner You is doing today. Think of a word or phrase for each letter.

I _____

N _____

N _____

E _____

R _____

M _____

E _____

PUSH MUTE

Below is a list of common temptations we can listen to instead of God's voice. Draw a "mute" line through the lies keeping you from trusting God. After figuratively pushing mute on these lies and silencing them, read the psalm on the next page OUT LOUD and literally claim every truth over yourself.

- 🔇 "anxiety"
- 🔇 "self-hatred"
- 🔇 "bitterness unforgiveness"
- 🔇 "temptation"
- 🔇 "peer pressure pleasing others"

- 🔇 "insecurity"
- 🔇 "judgment"
- 🔇 "unworthiness"
- 🔇 "distraction"
- 🔇 "fear"

PSALM 62: 5-8

Yes, my soul, find rest in God;
    my hope comes from him.
Truly he is my rock and my salvation;
    he is my fortress, I will not be shaken.
My salvation and my honor depend on God;
    he is my mighty rock, my refuge.
Trust in him at all times, you people;
    pour out your hearts to him,
    for God is our refuge.

LIVE LIKE CHRIST

If we want the change Jesus is brining to our hearts to stick, we must allow truth to spill over into our day-to-day lives. Use the following activities to discover and respond to where Jesus is taking you.

JOHN 10:4-10

> *"When he has brought out all his own, he goes on ahead of them, and his sheep follow him because they know his voice. But they will never follow a stranger; in fact, they will run away from him because they do not recognize a stranger's voice." Jesus used this figure of speech, but the Pharisees did not understand what he was telling them.*
>
> *Therefore Jesus said again, "Very truly I tell you, I am the gate for the sheep. All who have come before me are thieves and robbers, but the sheep have not listened to them. I am the gate; whoever enters through me will be saved. They will come in and go out, and find pasture. The thief comes only to steal and kill and destroy; I have come that they may have life, and have it to the full.*

Jesus, the Good Shepherd, tells us to follow His voice and run away from the voice of "strangers." What voices in your life should you be weary of listening to?

How can you practically prioritize listening to Jesus' voice?

FOLLOWING OUR SHEPHERD

Jesus uses the word picture of a shepherd calling to His sheep to illustrate how His followers are to know His voice and follow His lead. He offers this litmus test,

"The thief comes only to steal and kill and destroy; I have come that they may have life, and have it to the full." (John 10:10)

One way to discern God's voice is to ask yourself "Is the voice I am listening to leading me to have a more full life, or is it leading me to death and destruction?"

Name the characteristics of a person that garners your trust and following.

Describe a real life example of the thief and how you were or are misled by his voice.

THE SHEPHERD'S VOICE

Ask Jesus to speak to you today and spend some time listening for His voice. As words or phrases come to mind write them in the sheep.

THE BASEMENTS OF MY HEART:

The house and basements below represent the deepening levels of your heart. In each level write a word or phrase describing something that you are struggling to trust God with. The deeper the level, the harder it is for you to trust.

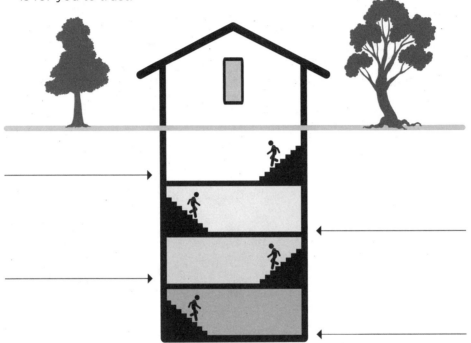

ACTION STEPS

Based on your basements, write down three action steps you want to pursue in the next week to better listen to the Good Shepherd's voice and trust Him with these inner areas.

ACTION STEP 1:

ACTION STEP 2:

ACTION STEP 3:

SESSION

CALL UPON
GOD

GATHER

Group Study

PREPARE!

Before you show up to your gathering, check in with yourself.

1 **THE TITLE OF TODAY IS:** _____

Title your day as if it were a chapter title in the book of your life. Be creative and not hasty. Think about the entire day or week you've had, not just the past hour.

2 **YOUR MOOD:** Circle all that apply.

3 **ENERGY LEVEL:** Mark along the line.

Blah . . .   Let's Do This!

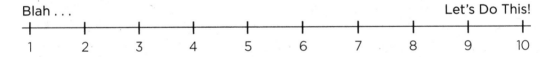

1   2   3   4   5   6   7   8   9   10

4 **I AM THANKFUL FOR:**

_____

_____

_____

_____

5 **MY HEART FEELS HEAVY BECAUSE:**

_____

_____

_____

_____

1 **MY ONE-WORD PRAYER FOR TODAY:** _____

Write out one word or sentence that could encapsulate a lot of what you are hoping to hear or discover today with God's help.

"ACTIONS ARE NOT IMPOSITIONS ON WHO WE ARE, BUT ARE **EXPRESSIONS** OF WHO WE ARE. THEY COME OUT OF OUR HEART AND THE INNER REALITIES IT SUPERVISES AND INTERACTS WITH."

—DALLAS WILLARD

GATHERING TRANSITION TIME (10 Minutes)

> **RELEVANT VERSES:**
> **JOHN** 15:1-17

Using only three words, write the answer to the following question and share with your group:

How would you describe your personal **Study & Seek** *time working through levels of listening for God's voice and trusting Him?*

_____ _____ _____

> *Share one or two action steps you wrote down in your STUDY & SEEK time. Allow your group to join you in living out these steps as your accountability partners.*

SESSION 3 **VIDEO** (25 Minutes)

Let's watch the video for this session and feel free to take notes below.

> **NOTES:**
> Divine encounters start with simple questions.

> You will miss God's plans if your life revolves around your own plans.

A Gardener is closest to the branches when He is pruning them.

The opposite of remaining is pretense.

Where are you looking for your source of life lately?

Our role is obedience. God is in control of the results.

WHAT'S GOD SAYING? (5 Minutes)

Take a minute on your own to look over your notes and write down what stands out, resonates, or challenges you most. Then we'll have one or two people briefly share.

_____

_____

_____

"WE OUGHT NOT
TO BE WEARY
OF DOING
LITTLE THINGS
FOR THE **LOVE**
OF GOD, WHO
REGARDS NOT
THE GREATNESS
OF THE WORK,
BUT THE **LOVE**
WITH WHICH IT
IS PERFORMED."

—BROTHER LAWRENCE

THINK BEFORE YOU SPEAK
(5 Minutes)

UNDERSTANDING RHYTHMS

Pick one person to read aloud to the group before you begin group discussion.

Discovering what we are abiding in is one thing. Actually shifting our hearts to instead remain in Jesus is a whole other thing. We have to incorporate new rhythms in our lives pointing us towards Jesus and helping us stay connected with Him. These rhythms are intentional practices, known as spiritual disciplines, that we work into our regular lives to help us better remain or abide in Jesus. They have no transformative power in-and-of themselves. In fact, when we make them into a meaningless ritual they do very little to shape our inner selves. They should instead be thought of as different forms of prayer (i.e. ways to connect with Jesus in relation-ship). When used as a means of relationship, they help to open our hearts to Jesus, the one who can transform us from the inside out. Think of them as paths leading you to your home in Jesus.

_____

_____

_____

_____

_____

In our **GROUP DISCUSSION**, we are going to explore together some rhythms you can incorporate into your everyday life. The list is not exhaustive but it can give you a good place to start.

GROUP DISCUSSION (30-40 Minutes)

Leader, read each numbered prompt out loud and ask the corresponding discussion question.

REMAIN

JOHN 15:1-5

I am the true vine, and my Father is the gardener. He cuts off every branch in me that bears no fruit, while every branch that does bear fruit he prunes so that it will be even more fruitful. You are already clean because of the word I have spoken to you. Remain in me, as I also remain in you. No branch can bear fruit by itself; it must remain in the vine. Neither can you bear fruit unless you remain in me. I am the vine; you are the branches. If you remain in me and I in you, you will bear much fruit; apart from me you can do nothing.

● How does this passage change replacing the word "remain" with "continue to be present" or "endure"?

1

FASTING

Matthew 4:4

Man shall not live on bread alone, but on every word that comes from the mouth of God.

● What are you willing to give up to spend more time with God's Word?

4

2

3

SERVING

Matthew 25:40

Truly I tell you, whatever you did for one of the least of these brothers and sisters of mine, you did for me.

● In what ways might Jesus consider someone to be "least of these"?

● How can we serve Jesus by serving the "least of these" in our own lives?

LISTENING

Luke 11:28

Blessed rather are those who hear the word of God and obey it.

● What do you find more difficult, to listen or to hear? What is the difference?

● If one goes to the head and one to the heart, which goes where and what does that have to do with blessing and obedience?

STUDYING

Romans 15:4

For everything . . . was written to teach us, so that through the endurance taught in the Scriptures and the encouragement they provide we might have hope.

- Do you resonate with having been taught endurance through the Scriptures? Why or why not?

- How might a long study of Scripture be more productive than looking for a quick answer or encouragement?

WORSHIPING

John 4:23

. . .true worshipers will worship the Father in the Spirit and in truth

- Describe a part of your daily life which could become an act of worship?

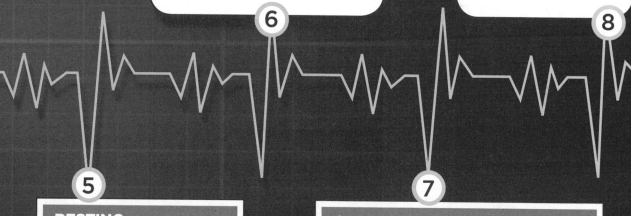

RESTING

Matthew 11:28

Come to me, all you who are weary and burdened, and I will give you rest.

- What is the difference between human rest and the rest Jesus offers?

QUIETING

Psalm 46:10

. . . Be still, and know that I am God

- What is the greatest obstacle you face for getting still—in any form?

- Why do you think "being" with God is often more of a concept than our reality?

- How does "being" with God increase our ability to know Him?

RECEIVE BLESSING
(5 Minutes)

Leader, have everyone sit with hands open, palms up. Read the following blessing over your group before closing in prayer.

May you experience overwhelming restoration in rhythm with Christ.

CLOSING PRAYER

Encourage the group to engage the personal study material throughout the week before your next gathering. Pray in whichever way best suits your group, and use this space to keep track of prayer requests and praises. Dismiss!

SESSION

CALL UPON
GOD

STUDY AND SEEK

Personal Study

WALK IN STEP

THE MOTIVATION OF SPIRITUAL RHYTHMS

In His most famous sermon, the Sermon on the Mount, Jesus takes a critical look at the spiritual rhythms of His day. Jesus points out it is not enough to simply practice these disciplines, but the true value of them comes when they are practiced with the right motives and heart. Many of those around Jesus were in the habit of using spiritual practices to make themselves feel good about their spiritual lives and look good in the eyes of others. Jesus suggests that in doing so they have stolen from themselves the greatest reward these practices can offer, opening one's heart to deeper connection with their Father in Heaven.

Read the the following passage three times:

- The first time, **underline** all the words and phrases that stand out to you.

- The second, **write** all the **questions** you have about the passage as they come up.

- The third time around, **circle** the **key words** or phrases God might be highlighting for you.

Afterward, work through the **PERSONAL INVENTORY** to help you think the connection between the passage and your current life experience.

MATTHEW 6:1-8, 16-18

¹ "Be careful not to practice your righteousness in front of others to be seen by them. If you do, you will have no reward from your Father in heaven.

² "So when you give to the needy, do not announce it with trumpets, as the hypocrites do in the synagogues and on the streets, to be honored by others. Truly I tell you, they have received their reward in full. ³ But when you give to the needy, do not let your left hand know what your right hand is doing, ⁴ so that your giving may be in secret. Then your Father, who sees what is done in secret, will reward you.

⁵ "And when you pray, do not be like the hypocrites, for they love to pray standing in the synagogues and on the street corners to be seen by others. Truly I tell you, they have received their reward in full. ⁶ But when you pray, go into your room, close the door and pray to your Father, who is unseen. Then your Father, who sees what is done in secret, will reward you. ⁷ And when you pray, do not keep on babbling like pagans, for they think they will be heard because of their many words. ⁸ Do not be like them, for your Father knows what you need before you ask him…

¹⁶ "When you fast, do not look somber as the hypocrites do, for they disfigure their faces to show others they are fasting. Truly I tell you, they have received their reward in full. ¹⁷ But when you fast, put oil on your head and wash your face, ¹⁸ so that it will not be obvious to others that you are fasting, but only to your Father, who is unseen; and your Father, who sees what is done in secret, will reward you."

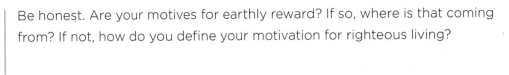

▶ PERSONAL INVENTORY

Spend some time in a gut level heart check with God. Take stock of where you're at—healthy and not-so-healthy.

HOW AM I PRACTICING RIGHTEOUSNESS?

Be honest. Are your motives for earthly reward? If so, where is that coming from? If not, how do you define your motivation for righteous living?

WHAT MOTIVATES ME TO HELP?

Consider your heart carefully. When you give to the needy—in time, in resources, in prayer—what is your expectation in return?

Are you satisfied giving in anonymity? Why or why not?

How does your attitude need to change to offer service for the sake of honoring God and caring for others?

WHY DO I PRAY, REALLY?

Consider when you pray in front of others. Do you wonder what they think of what you are saying, how you are saying it, why you are saying it? How do these distractions affect your communication with God?

Are your prayers different in front of others than when you are alone, in private? Describe.

When you pray alone, in private, where is your prayer coming from? Personal need? Desire? Ambition? Concern?

Is your motivation for prayer to be closer to God and to seek alignment with His will? Describe how your prayer life would change if you intentionally and deliberately considered why you are praying before you began.

WHAT DO I GIVE UP AND WHY?

Fasting is an act of personal sacrifice. It is commonly referred to and practiced in Scripture but is less common today. Consider what you can give up, or fast from for a period of time so God can fill that space in your life. The goal is not to out-fast someone else. The goal is to grow more deeply aware of your dependence on God and how trustworthy He is with your every need.

What can you give up or fast from this week?

List the ways fasting from _____ will provide space for God.

How deep are you willing to go in sacrifice?

How much are you willing to suffer?

"ULTIMATELY, THE GOAL OF PERSONAL BIBLE STUDY IS A TRANSFORMED LIFE AND A DEEP AND ABIDING **RELATIONSHIP** WITH JESUS CHRIST."

—KAY ARTHUR

PSALM 46: 1-3

God is our refuge and strength,
   an ever-present help in trouble.
Therefore we will not fear, though the earth give way
   and the mountains fall into the heart of the sea,
though its waters roar and foam
   and the mountains quake with their surging.

▶ MY REFUGE AND STRENGTH

Write a short prayer telling God how you need Him to be your refuge and strength today.

ROMANS 12:1-2

> Therefore, I urge you, brothers and sisters, in view of God's mercy, to offer your bodies as a living sacrifice, holy and pleasing to God—this is your true and proper worship. [2] Do not conform to the pattern of this world, but be transformed by the renewing of your mind. Then you will be able to test and approve what God's will is—his good, pleasing and perfect will.

▶ *RENEWING OF YOUR MIND*

Throughout Romans, Paul has sought to unify the church in Rome by unpacking how we are all helplessly broken and desperately in need of Jesus' amazing love and grace. Our own strength and merit cannot save us. Furthermore, His love and grace alone can give new life, transform us, bring us together as one family, and give us a new future of joining God in His great purposes. What then is our role? Romans 12 explains we have the choice of alignment. Rather than aligning ourselves with the *patterns of this world*, Paul urges believers to give over their *bodies as living sacrifices* to God. In doing so, they intentionally align themselves with the current of the Holy Spirit's transformative work in their minds (inner beliefs). Using one's free will to intentionally choose alignment is like opening sails to discern and catch the momentum of where God is moving.

In what ways do you notice yourself conforming to the pattern of this world?

What do you think it means to offer your body as a living sacrifice?

LIVE LIKE CHRIST

If we want the change Jesus is brining to our hearts to stick, we must allow truth to spill over into our day-to-day lives. Use the following activity to discover and respond to where Jesus is taking you.

Ask God what three areas of your mind (your inner beliefs) He wants to bring more alignment in. Spend some time just listening and remaining in His presence. List them below.

> *Some examples of inner beliefs God may want to help you align with Him may include your belief about: who God is, how good God is, how good God's plans are for your life, what the good plans look like, who you are, how loved you are, how forgiven you are, how valuable you are, how God is with you, etc.)*

_____

_____

_____

_____

_____

_____

ACTION STEPS

Based on your personal inventory and what God has laid on your heart to come into alignment with Him, write three action steps you want to pursue in the next week that you believe will bring you into rhythm with Christ.

ACTION STEP 1:

ACTION STEP 2:

ACTION STEP 3:

COME AND
PRAY

GATHER

Group Study

PREPARE!

Before you show up to your gathering, check in with yourself.

① THE TITLE OF TODAY IS: _____

Title your day as if it were a chapter title in the book of your life. Be creative and not hasty. Think about the entire day or week you've had, not just the past hour.

② YOUR MOOD: Circle all that apply.

③ ENERGY LEVEL: Mark along the line.

Blah . . .   Let's Do This!

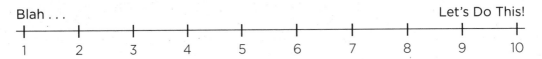

1   2   3   4   5   6   7   8   9   10

④ I AM THANKFUL FOR:

_____

_____

_____

_____

⑤ MY HEART FEELS HEAVY BECAUSE:

_____

_____

_____

_____

① MY ONE-WORD PRAYER FOR TODAY: _____

Write out one word or sentence that could encapsulate a lot of what you are hoping to hear or discover today with God's help.

"OF ALL SPIRITUAL DISCIPLINES **PRAYER** IS THE MOST CENTRAL BECAUSE IT USHERS US INTO **PERPETUAL COMMUNION** WITH THE FATHER."

—RICHARD FOSTER

GATHERING TRANSITION TIME (10 Minutes)

> **RELEVANT VERSES:**
> **LUKE** 3:21-22
> **LUKE** 4:1-2
> **LUKE** 5:15-16
> **LUKE** 9:18
> **LUKE** 11:1-4

Using only three words, write the answer to the following question:

How would you describe your personal Study & Seek time discovering new rhythms of connection to Christ?

_____ _____ _____

Briefly share your words with your group.

SESSION 4 VIDEO (20 Minutes)

Let's watch the video for this session and feel free to take notes below.

> **NOTES:**
> Prayer is spending time with the one who loves you most.

Jesus was given His identity, worth, and position as He was praying.

In Christ, God's words are for you too:

- *You are my child,*

- *I love you,*

- *With you I am already well pleased.*

What you do in private spaces equips you for public places.

We pray so that we will do what Jesus did, have what Jesus has, and begin to want what Jesus wants.

Through His prayer, Jesus reveals to us what we really need.

WHAT'S GOD SAYING? (3 Minutes)

Take a minute on your own to look over your notes and write down what stands out, resonates, or challenges you most. Then we'll have one or two people briefly share.

_____

_____

_____

"**PRAYER** IS
NOT WHAT GOD
WANTS *FROM*
YOU, IT IS WHAT
GOD WANTS
FOR YOU."

—MEGAN

THINK BEFORE YOU SPEAK
(5 Minutes)

Pick one person to read aloud to the group before you begin group discussion.

The first three chapters of Luke demonstrate prayer as common communication with God. Jesus' mother Mary prays a beautiful prayer in chapter 1, before Jesus is born. Chapter 2 is filed with a host of angels praising God, shepherds praising God for the baby born, Simeon taking baby Jesus at the temple and praying thanks to God while offering blessings, and finally a prayer warrior named Anna "coming up to them . . . gave thanks to God and spoke about the child to all who were looking forward to the redemption of Jerusalem." Every prayer began with gratitude and recognition of God's love and faithfulness through Jesus. But in chapter 3, Luke introduces Jesus as an adult, being baptized and praying. Verses 21–22 reveal what was perhaps most important to Jesus, communication with God: "And as he was praying, heaven opened and the Holy Spirit descended on him in bodily form like a dove. And a voice came from heaven: "You are my son, whom I love; with you I am well pleased."

Prayer is essential in Scripture and in our lives. Let's consider how we experience it in discussion together.

In this week's **GROUP DISCUSSION,** we are going to look at **Matthew 9:1-13** when Jesus teaches His disciples how to pray and dig into what we know of prayer and how this communication with God reveals His love for us.

GROUP DISCUSSION (30-40 Minutes)

Leader, read each numbered prompt out loud and ask the corresponding discussion question.

MATTHEW 6:9-13

"This, then, is how you should pray: "'Our Father in heaven, hallowed be your name, your kingdom come, your will be done, on earth as it is in heaven. Give us today our daily bread. And forgive us our debts, as we also have forgiven our debtors. And lead us not into temptation, but deliver us from the evil one.

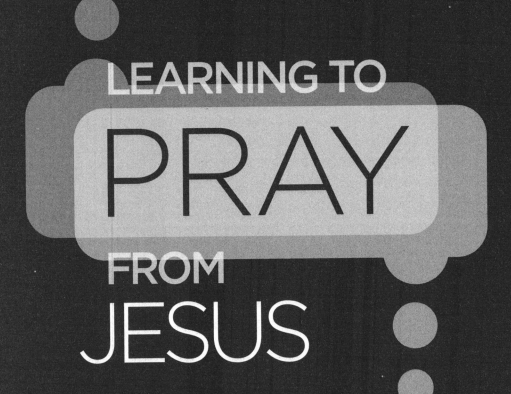

LEARNING TO PRAY FROM JESUS

FATHER, HALLOWED BE YOUR NAME

Jesus began His prayers naming who He was speaking with in both salutation and adoration. He grounded His prayer in acknowledging God as Father, deserving hallowed (set apart, holy) recognition.

- **When you think about the last few times you've prayed, who was really at the center of your prayer?**

KINGDOM COME, YOUR WILL BE DONE

ver took His eye off the prize-eternity with God. He never once considered anything He
r desired apart from God's Kingdom fully restored. He tells us to remember what it's all for.

**oes your understanding of praying with your whole heart change if your prayers are
to be about God's will being done, not yours?**

GIVE US TODAY OUR DAILY BREAD

After Jesus teaches us to pray for God's Kingdom to come and will to be done He invites us to address our needs just for today.

- **When was the last time you thought only about today? Don't answer that. It was never. But what if today was all you had to pray about and focus on? What changes in your heart? In your prayer?**

VE OUR DEBTS AS WE FORGIVE OTHERS

forgiveness. As we receive it, we're humbled. Humility is required for giving forgiveness
reely as it has been received.

**describes asking for forgiveness as we are forgiving others. What is the intended
ation?**

s humility so hard?

LEAD US FROM TEMPTATION, DELIVER US FROM THE EVIL ONE

Before we can resist, combat, and overcome our struggles, we have to acknowledge who is greater, how great He is, surrender our desires to His will, ask for what we need today, find forgiveness as we forgive, and follow His lead.

- **Why do you think Jesus placed temptation and deliverance last in His example of prayer?**
- **What priority do you give temptations and the need for deliverance in your prayers?**

RECEIVE BLESSING
(5 Minutes)

Leader, have everyone sit with hands open, palms up. Read the following blessing over your group before closing in prayer.

> May you know that in Christ, without question, you are known and heard by God, who loves you as His child.

CLOSING PRAYER (5 Minutes)

Encourage the group to engage the personal study material throughout the week before your next gathering. Pray in whichever way best suits your group, and use this space to keep track of prayer requests and praises. Dismiss!

COME AND
PRAY

STUDY AND SEEK

Personal Study

WALK IN STEP

THE CONTEXT OF A PASSAGE

The word *gospel* means *good news*. The four Gospels (Matthew, Mark, Luke, & John) tell the good news about Jesus' life, death, and resurrection while He physically walked the Earth. A Gospel, in the Biblical sense, is also its own unique genre of writing. Not only do Gospels record actual historical events, they also have intentional meaning for the reader to uncover. The writers of the Gospels were inspired by God and very meticulous about what stories and teachings they included and in what order. When wanting to understand the context of a story from the Gospels, it can be helpful to compare the same story in other gospels while considering the variance in details each author felt compelled to include or not.

Read the following passage three times:

- The first time, **underline** all the words and phrases that stand out to you.

- The second, **write** all the **questions** you have about the passage as they come up.

- The third time around, **circle** the **key words** or phrases God might be highlighting for you.

Afterward, go through the Context Worksheet to help you think the passage through.

LUKE 10:38-42

[38] As Jesus and his disciples were on their way, he came to a village where a woman named Martha opened her home to him. [39] She had a sister called Mary, who sat at the Lord's feet listening to what he said. [40] But Martha was distracted by all the preparations that had to be made. She came to him and asked, "Lord, don't you care that my sister has left me to do the work by myself? Tell her to help me!"

[41] "Martha, Martha," the Lord answered, "you are worried and upset about many things, [42] but few things are needed—or indeed only one. Mary has chosen what is better, and it will not be taken away from her."

CONTEXT WORKSHEET

▶ *PASSAGE:*

LUKE 10:38-42

GENRE OF THIS PASSAGE:	CHARACTERS IN PASSAGE:
Gospel	*Jesus, Martha, and Mary*

PASSAGE DIRECTLY BEFORE:	ACTION NOTES:
Look up and write a short summary of Luke 10:25-37:	Briefly note the actions of each character in the passage.
How might this deepen my understanding of the passage?	How does the action of each character reflect the focus of their heart?

What do you notice about Jesus and His character from the story? What might be one lesson Luke intended to share with this story?

▶ HOW DO YOU PRAY?

If prayer is connecting with the one who loves you most, write down the five practices that help you feel most connected to God. Think of both traditional prayer practices and the unconventional and unique activities and experiences that help you connect with God.

1 _____

_____

_____

2 _____

_____

_____

3 _____

_____

_____

4 _____

_____

_____

5 _____

_____

_____

▶ CAST YOUR CARES

Your heavenly Father loves you so much and cares about your needs. Showing our true, honest self to Him in prayer is both a safe and powerful practice. The Bible says to "Cast all your anxiety on him because he cares for you." (1 Peter 5:7) Write a letter to your Heavenly Father offering Him everything going on inside you right now.

Dear Heavenly Father,

▶ PRACTICING THE PRESENCE

Look up and read 1 Thessalonians 5:16-24.
What makes connecting with God in all circumstances challenging?

Paul knows living the life God is calling us to can only be powered by continual communion with God. This is why he encourages the church in Thessalonica to *pray continually* among other perpetual practices of rejoicing and giving thanks which help to create this connection. This practice of staying aware of, present with, and dependent on God throughout your day is commonly known as *practicing the presence of God*. In doing so we tend to the fire that the Spirit is building inside us, not *quenching* it, but fueling it as the Spirit uses it to move, guide, and work through us. We will also be able to discern the words of God coming through others, known as *prophecy*. When someone thinks of a prophet today, they think of someone who foretells the future. Biblically, however, a prophet is a person who speaks for someone else. A "spokesperson," not a clairvoyant. Simply, a biblical prophet is a person declaring the words of God. Prophets were used by God to communicate His truth. In all this God will continue to shape us more like Jesus (*sanctify* us).

Where have you noticed yourself ignoring or moving against what the Holy Spirit wants to do in your heart? How could you better tend to this fire He is creating in you?

LIVE LIKE CHRIST

PRAYER BRACELET

Create a string bracelet to tie around your wrist as a reminder that your Heavenly Father is with you and that your soul thirsts for Him. (Psalm 42:1) As you notice it throughout your day, use it as a reminder of His presence. Let it lead you to practice the presence of God. Your bracelet can be as simple as a piece of string or can be something more complex that you find online.

ACTION STEPS

Based on your learning and experiences from this session, write down three action steps you want to pursue in the next week to grow stronger in prayer and closer to God through it.

ACTION STEP 1:

ACTION STEP 2:

ACTION STEP 3:

SEEK **HIM** WITH ALL YOUR **HEART**

GATHER

Group Study

PREPARE!

Before you show up to your gathering, check in with yourself.

❶ THE TITLE OF TODAY IS: _____

Title your day as if it were a chapter title in the book of your life. Be creative and not hasty. Think about the entire day or week you've had, not just the past hour.

❷ YOUR MOOD: Circle all that apply.

❸ ENERGY LEVEL: Mark along the line.

Blah . . .   Let's Do This!

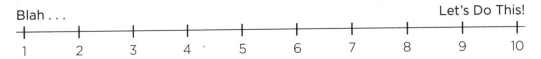

1   2   3   4   5   6   7   8   9   10

❹ I AM THANKFUL FOR:

_____

_____

_____

_____

❺ MY HEART FEELS HEAVY BECAUSE:

_____

_____

_____

_____

❻ MY ONE-WORD PRAYER FOR TODAY: _____

Write out one word or sentence that could encapsulate a lot of what you are hoping to hear or discover today with God's help.

"NOTHING IN OR OF THIS WORLD MEASURES UP TO THE SIMPLE **PLEASURE** OF EXPERIENCING THE **PRESENCE** OF GOD."

—A.W. TOZER

GATHERING TRANSITION TIME (10 Minutes)

> ### *RELEVANT VERSES:*
> **JEREMIAH** 29:13
> **EPHESIANS** 3:14-21

Using only three words, write the answer to the following question:

How would you describe your personal Study & Seek *time learning about prayer and the priority of ongoing conversation with God?*

_____ _____ _____

Briefly share your words with your group.

SESSION 5 **VIDEO** (15 Minutes)

Let's watch the video for this session and feel free to take notes below.

> ### *NOTES:*
> God wants to flip-flop our expectations.

From our heart springs our thoughts, emotions, and actions.

Our heart is like a cup.

Even wonderful byproducts make for crummy goals.

Seek God in everything and everyone.

Seeing the best in others means seeing God's image in them.

WHAT'S GOD SAYING? (3 Minutes)

Take a minute on your own to look over your notes and write down what stands out, resonates, or challenges you most. Then we'll have one or two people briefly share.

_____

_____

_____

"**SEEK** GOD = **FIND**
GOD, PERIOD."

—MEGAN

THINK BEFORE YOU SPEAK
(15 Minutes)

Leader, open your Bible and read Psalm 63 out loud to the group.

WHAT'S IT ABOUT?

Pick one person to read the following to the group.

The concept of seeking God can become too undefined for us to really take hold of and run with. This is normal. But we are not left without examples of what seeking God looks like.

David, the one often referred to as "a man after God's own heart" spent a good portion of his psalms writing in the throes of seeking God. Psalm 63 is perhaps the most significant of his psalms about seeking after God. We come to see through David's somewhat internal dialogue that for him, seeking after God means to have an intimate personal relationship with Him. He desires this closeness to God so much he compares it to thirst (63:1). David seeks satisfaction, something we all relate to, but he has a different perspective—seeking God IS what satisfies him. He finds fullness in thinking about God, praising Him, remembering all He has done for him. David seeks God because David cannot imagine any other anything that will fill him up mentally, physically, spiritually, emotionally, or literally than God.

_____

_____

_____

In our **GROUP DISCUSSION** this week, we are going to focus on what Scripture means when it refers to "being filled by the Spirit" and "the filling God in us." It is no wonder we might struggle to seek God with our whole heart if we don't truly understand what for.

GROUP DISCUSSION (30-40 Minutes)

Leader, read each numbered prompt out loud and ask the corresponding discussion question.

1

POWER AND FAITH

I pray that out of his glorious riches he may strengthen you with power through his Spirit in your inner being, so that Christ may dwell in your hearts through faith.
—Ephesians 3:16-17

. . . .

Dive into the connections between what the Spirit gives us, from where, and how it manifests through us. What does it mean and practically look like for Christ to dwell in our hearts?

2

SEEK AND TRUST

When we seek Jesus and put our trust in Him, we are found in Him, meaning we are offered His life, righteousness, position, and are welcomed as God's children just as He is.

. . . .

Over the last few weeks, where have you felt most at home with Jesus (i.e. loved by Him, at peace with Him, connected to Him, etc.)?

UNDERSTANDING GOD'S

3 MEASURE

. . . and to know this love that surpasses knowledge—that you may be filled to the measure of all the fullness of God.
—Ephesians 3:19

Have you ever felt the love of Jesus surpass knowledge or your ability to comprehend it? Share with the group your experience of "being filled to the measure of all the fullness of God."

4 JESUS

Consider how it feels when we are spent, parched, lost, dried up from pouring out and in desperate need for refreshment.

Look up and read:
Psalm 81:10, Psalm 103:5, Psalm 107:9

Notice the language the Psalmist uses and how "what" God fills us with is simply "good things."

In what ways can you see God's filling of good things in your life?

How do you need His filling right now?

Who receives when you pour good things out?

5 FILLED TO OVERFLOW

But God is not done! The beauty of being strengthened with power in our inner being and being filled to the measure of the fullness of God is that His love is abounding. Imagine our heart being filled with God's infinite love gushing into it and overflowing out of it. Our actions can have impact as we overflow Jesus' love to others through us.

How have you noticed the Holy Spirit strengthening you with power in your inner being over the course of this study?

How specifically is God leading you to overflow? Does someone specific come to mind? What would it look like for you to overflow Christ's indwelling love to them instead of loving them with your own strength?

FILLING

RECEIVE BLESSING
(5 Minutes)

Leader, have everyone sit with hands open, palms up. Read the following blessing over your group before closing in prayer.

> May you be filled to the measure of all the fullness of God so that you can overflow Christ's love to a thirsty world.

CLOSING PRAYER

Encourage the group to engage the personal study material throughout the week before your next gathering. Pray in whichever way best suits your group, and use this space to keep track of prayer requests and praises. Dismiss!

SEEK HIM WITH ALL YOUR HEART

STUDY AND SEEK

Personal Study

WALK IN STEP

THE HOLY SPIRIT

Shortly after He ascended into Heaven, Jesus sends to His disciples "another advocate to help you and be with you forever" just as He promised in John 14:16. During the Jewish holiday of Pentecost the Holy Spirit arrived and filled the disciples in dramatic fashion. The filling of the Holy Spirit is promised to all who put their faith in Jesus. Romans 8:11 points out how powerful this truth is, "The Spirit of God, who raised Jesus from the dead, lives in you. And just as God raised Christ Jesus from the dead, he will give life to your mortal bodies by this same Spirit living within you." When God's Spirit lives in us, we are filled with His power to accomplish the good purposes He has for us. Through the Spirit we are enabled with certain gifts "given for the common good" of the Church and those He calls us to serve.

Read the following passage three times:

- The first time, **underline** all the words and phrases that stand out to you.

- The second, **write** all the **questions** you have about the passage as they come up.

- The third time around, **circle** the **key words** or phrases God might be highlighting for you.

Afterward, spend some time *Praying Through Scripture*.

ACTS 2:1-12

[1] When the day of Pentecost came, they were all together in one place. [2] Suddenly a sound like the blowing of a violent wind came from heaven and filled the whole house where they were sitting. [3] They saw what seemed to be tongues of fire that separated and came to rest on each of them. [4] All of them were filled with the Holy Spirit and began to speak in other tongues as the Spirit enabled them.

[5] Now there were staying in Jerusalem God-fearing Jews from every nation under heaven. [6] When they heard this sound, a crowd came together in bewilderment, because each one heard their own language being spoken. [7] Utterly amazed, they asked: "Aren't all these who are speaking Galileans? [8] Then how is it that each of us hears them in our native language? [9] Parthians, Medes and Elamites; residents of Mesopotamia, Judea and Cappadocia, Pontus and Asia, [10] Phrygia and Pamphylia, Egypt and the parts of Libya near Cyrene; visitors from Rome [11] (both Jews and converts to Judaism); Cretans and Arabs—we hear them declaring the wonders of God in our own tongues!" [12] Amazed and perplexed, they asked one another, "What does this mean?"

▶ PRAYING THROUGH SCRIPTURE

SEEK out and write down three observations that stand out to you from this story in Acts. For each observation, spend a few minutes seeking God by listening to Him and asking, "Lord, what truth do you want to show me from this observation?" Write those truths God helps you to FIND below each observation. Finally write three practical ways you can APPLY those principles to your own life.

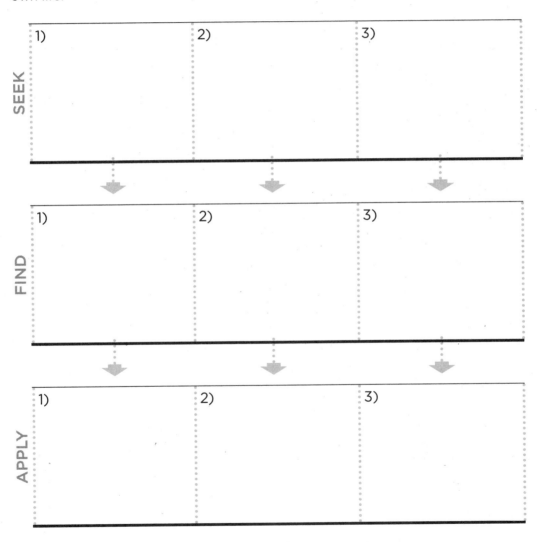

LUKE 6:43-45

"No good tree bears bad fruit, nor does a bad tree bear good fruit. Each tree is recognized by its own fruit. People do not pick figs from thornbushes, or grapes from briers. A good man brings good things out of the good stored up in his heart, and an evil man brings evil things out of the evil stored up in his heart. For the mouth speaks what the heart is full of.

▶ RECOGNIZING THE ROOTS

● What has filled up your heart (or your attention) lately?

● How is what you are seeking with your heart bringing about both good and evil in your life?

Jesus' teaching in Luke 6:43-45 is pretty straight forward. Not only are the things we fill our heart with insufficient in light of the filling God offers us, they also result in undesirable words and actions to overflow out of our life. This is why Proverbs 4:23 says, "Above all else, guard your heart, for everything you do flows from it." The *evil fruit* that overflows from our hearts comes from deep rooted beliefs that cause us all to live selfishly. Like a weed, if we try to deal only with what we see above ground, the issue will grow back in one way or another. Jesus desires to help us remove these evil root beliefs and replace them with a healthy seed of truth that we can tend to as it grows.

● Where do you think our core beliefs come from? How can tracing back negative core beliefs be helpful in uprooting them?

▶ THE SEEKING EQUATION

This week we learned about Jeremiah 29:13 and how God says, "You will seek me and find me when you seek me with all your heart." Take some time here, really dig into the honest place of vulnerability and fill in the chart below. How does everything change when God is who and what we seek?

WHAT MY HEART SEEKS	WHY I AM SEEKING	WHAT CHANGES WHEN I SEEK GOD
affirmation	I feel overlooked	I find confidence

LIVE LIKE CHRIST

Use this chart to practice reframing your thought pattern. Seek the character and heart and promise of God and you will learn to trust Him over any circumstance or question or doubt life presents.

I TRUST GOD BECAUSE HE IS . . .	
LOOK UP	**CHARACTER OF GOD**
Malachi 3:6	*unchangeable*
Romans 9:15-16	
1 John 4:7	
Psalm 139 Jeremiah 23:23-34	
Isaiah 46:9-19	

ACTION STEPS

Based on what you discovered of God's character, write out three practical and specific action steps you will pursue this week to seek him with all your heart and increase your trust exponentially.

ACTION STEP 1:

ACTION STEP 2:

ACTION STEP 3:

"**AGAPE** IS SOMETHING OF THE UNDERSTANDING, CREATIVE, REDEMPTIVE GOODWILL FOR ALL MEN. IT IS A **LOVE** THAT SEEKS NOTHING IN RETURN. IT IS AN **OVERFLOWING** LOVE; IT'S WHAT THEOLOGIANS WOULD CALL THE LOVE OF GOD **WORKING** IN THE LIVES OF MEN. AND WHEN YOU RISE TO LOVE ON THIS LEVEL, YOU BEGIN TO LOVE MEN, NOT BECAUSE THEY ARE LIKEABLE, BUT BECAUSE GOD LOVES THEM."

—MARTIN LUTHER KING JR.

SAYING YES TO GOD

GATHER

Group Study

PREPARE!

Before you show up to your gathering, check in with yourself.

1 THE TITLE OF TODAY IS: _____

Title your day as if it were a chapter title in the book of your life. Be creative and not hasty. Think about the entire day or week you've had, not just the past hour.

2 YOUR MOOD: Circle all that apply.

3 ENERGY LEVEL: Mark along the line.

Blah . . .   Let's Do This!

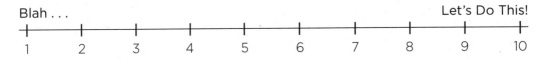

1   2   3   4   5   6   7   8   9   10

4 I AM THANKFUL FOR:

_____

_____

_____

_____

5 MY HEART FEELS HEAVY BECAUSE:

_____

_____

_____

_____

1 MY ONE-WORD PRAYER FOR TODAY: _____

Write out one word or sentence that could encapsulate a lot of what you are hoping to hear or discover today with God's help.

"I USED TO THINK
YOU HAD TO BE
SPECIAL FOR GOD
TO **USE** YOU, BUT
NOW I KNOW
YOU SIMPLY NEED
TO SAY **YES**."

—BOB GOFF

CELEBRATE!

▶ **RELEVANT VERSES:**
JEREMIAH 29:11-14
MATTHEW 28:16-20
ACTS 1-2
ROMANS 8:28-29

For our final gathering today let's take some time to remember and celebrate all God has done.

GATHERING TRANSITION TIME (10 Minutes)

Using only three words, write the answer to the following question:
What has been the most valuable session, discussion, teaching, or personal revelation from this study for you?

_____   _____   _____

Briefly share your words with your group.

SESSION 6 **VIDEO** (15 Minutes)

Let's watch the video for this session and feel free to take notes below.

▶ **NOTES:**
Every "Yes" is a "No" and every "No" is a "Yes."

Sin: saying "No" to God for the sake of saying "Yes" to something else.

Jesus ascended so that He could descend to dwell within us.

What we do actually matters.

The good God does *in* you is meant to go *through* you and onto someone else.

Jesus is up to whatever you are up to by the power of the Holy Spirit inside you.

WHAT'S GOD SAYING? (3 Minutes)

Take a minute on your own to look over your notes and write down what stands out, resonates, or challenges you most. Then we'll have one or two people briefly share.

_____

_____

_____

"THE BEST 'YES'
YOU'LL FIND IS
ANYTHING HE IS
ASKING OF YOU."

—MEGAN

THINK BEFORE YOU SPEAK
(5 Minutes)

Pick one person to read out loud:

UNDERSTANDING THE GREAT COMMISSION

Jesus' words in Matthew 28, known as the Great Commission, gets pegged as a passage promoting only evangelism (sharing the Gospel with others). Even though this is a huge part of this passage there is so much more to it. Jesus calls His followers to make disciples and baptize them. Dallas Willard notes that this means "immerse them together in the presence of the Trinity, the Father, the Son, and the Holy Spirit. Yes, baptize them in the name, but, dear friends, that doesn't just mean getting them wet while you say those names. It means to immerse them in the Reality."[1] Furthermore, we are to teach them to obey Jesus and His commands. This means that we are not making disciples of ourselves but helping to make disciples of Jesus. Jesus tells us that He will be with us always indicating that this disciple making work comes through the power of His Holy Spirit working through us.

_____

_____

_____

_____

_____

In this week's **GROUP DISCUSSION**, we are going to look at the Great Commission. As we've learned, God's plan is to make each of us more like Christ, so let's bring it all together this week and put what we've learned in to action!

Leader, read each numbered prompt out loud and ask the corresponding discussion question.

SAY YES TO SHARING

MEET THEM WHERE THEY ARE

When Jesus calls us to *go*, He is calling us to reflect His pursuit of humanity as we seek them out in love. This means we are to meet people where they are at, without judgment or condemnation. Like Jesus we are to see the image of God in everyone and invite them to meet the One who can shape them to become who they were always intended to be.

- **What is so powerful about meeting people where they are at?**
- **What does this look like practically?**

2 JESUS' COMMAND

Then the eleven disciples went to Galilee, to the mountain where Jesus had told them to go. When they saw him, they worshiped him; but some doubted. Then Jesus came to them and said, "All authority in heaven and on earth has been given to me. Therefore go and make disciples of all nations, baptizing them in the name of the Father and of the Son and of the Holy Spirit, and teaching them to obey everything I have commanded you. And surely I am with you always, to the very end of the age."

—Matthew 28:16-20

- **What do you think is the connection between Jesus having all authority and commanding us to make disciples?**

TRUST IS EVERYTHING

Throughout this study we heard about and discussed God's good plans for each of us and how those plans are to make us more like Christ. Go back to the first page of this study now. Select a volunteer to read The Gospel out loud to the group—this will be your third reading of the gospel.

- **Based on everything you have learned in this study, and the truth that is the gospel, why is trust so vital to sharing the good news of Jesus and saying "Yes!" to whatever God asks of us?**

5 IMMERSED IN TRUTH

As Dallas Willard notes, our baptism is not just with water but in the reality of who God is. This means we are helping others to immerse themselves in the life of Christ, love of the Father, power of the Spirit, and so much more. By this baptism we offer people the hope and future found in God's plans (Jeremiah 29:11) for their life.

- **How have you noticed your own baptism into the reality of who God is?**
- **What might it look like to help others enter into this reality?**

4 WALK IN STEP

By helping others immerse in this reality, we are showing them how to get caught up in the flow of what God is already doing. Teaching them to obey means teaching them to walk in step with Jesus' Spirit and move in partnership with His current. In this we invite them to join us on the ongoing journey of saying, "Yes" to walking in step with Jesus' Spirit.

- **Based on what you've learned in this study, how would you teach someone to walk in step with Jesus' Spirit?**

RECEIVE BLESSING
(5 Minutes)

Leader, have everyone sit with hands open, palms up. Read the following blessing over your group before closing in prayer.

> May today mark the day you say "Yes!" to God's invitation to call upon Him, come and pray to Him, and seek to find Him with all your heart. May you learn to walk in step with His Spirit and obediently say "Yes" to the adventure of trusting Him and the good plans He has for your life!

CLOSING PRAYER

Encourage the group to finish strong and complete the personal study work this week.

Take intentional time this week to share all the praises and answered prayers throughout this study. Share with one another ongoing prayer requests. But most importantly this week, commit to praying for the adventure each of you has ahead as you are made more like Christ daily!

SESSION

SAYING YES TO
GOD

STUDY AND SEEK

Personal Study

> *GO AT YOUR OWN PACE DOING A LITTLE AT A TIME, OR ALL AT ONCE.*

WALK IN STEP

STARTING WITH SCRIPTURE

All throughout this study, our starting point has been God's written words. This is to build in us the discipline of recognizing that God is already moving and helping us to identify how He is inviting us to join Him. In the next passage the prophet Isaiah was called to join in with God and what He was up to. Isaiah knew He was not worthy to be in the presence of God, let alone work alongside Him. But God cleanses Isaiah, pointing forward to the ultimate cleansing that would come to us all through Jesus.

Read the the following passage three times:

- The first time, **underline** all the words and phrases that stand out to you.

- The second, **write** all the **questions** you have about the passage as they come up.

- The third time around, **circle** the **key words** or phrases God might be highlighting for you.

Afterward, take some time to S.T.U.D.Y. the passage . . .

ISAIAH 6:1-8

[1] In the year that King Uzziah died, I saw the Lord, high and exalted, seated on a throne; and the train of his robe filled the temple. [2] Above him were seraphim, each with six wings: With two wings they covered their faces, with two they covered their feet, and with two they were flying. [3] And they were calling to one another:

"Holy, holy, holy is the Lord Almighty;

the whole earth is full of his glory."

[4] At the sound of their voices the doorposts and thresholds shook and the temple was filled with smoke.

5 "Woe to me!" I cried. "I am ruined! For I am a man of unclean lips, and I live among a people of unclean lips, and my eyes have seen the King, the Lord Almighty."

6 Then one of the seraphim flew to me with a live coal in his hand, which he had taken with tongs from the altar. 7 With it he touched my mouth and said, "See, this has touched your lips; your guilt is taken away and your sin atoned for."

8 Then I heard the voice of the Lord saying, "Whom shall I send? And who will go for us?"

And I said, "Here am I. Send me!"

▶ GO WITH THE GOSPEL

Turn to the beginning of your study guide (page iv) and read through the gospel again. Sit with the truth of the Good News for a few minutes asking God who He might want you to share His story of redemption with. Write down the name/names of who He reveals in the arrow below. Then make a plan to actually "GO" and share the gospel with that person!

▶ MOVING ONWARD AND UPWARD!

Look back on the early parts of this study and consider how you began your journey of trust in God's good plans for you. Write a single sentence that captures it in the first space below. Then write another sentence in the second space that captures where the adventure of trusting God has brought you.

⬤ I was . . .

⬤ I am now . . .

HOW YOU HAVE GROWN

Write a short thank you note to God for how you have seen Him grow you over the course of this study. Let this be a prayer of gratitude and acknowledgment. You may also consider writing a thank you note to any person who shared the gospel with you throughout your lifetime.

_____

_____

_____

_____

_____

PHILIPPIANS 1:3-6

> *I thank my God every time I remember you. In all my prayers for all of you, I always pray with joy because of your partnership in the gospel from the first day until now, being confident of this, that he who began a good work in you will carry it on to completion until the day of Christ Jesus.*

How is this prayer encouraging to you? What is it like to know that Jesus will continue the good work He has done in you throughout this study?

GOD IS FAITHFUL TO OUR YES

When you say "yes" to God, He is faithful to follow through with His promise to guide and love you. Spend some time thanking Him for His faithfulness to you throughout this study.

In the space below, write three of these ways you have seen God be faithful when you have said "YES!" to Him.

1. _____
2. _____
3. _____

LIVE
LIKE
CHRIST

God is not done! He wants to move you beyond where you are today and on to many other places of growth.

Ask God for one word that describes how He wants to grow you in this next season and write it on the line below.

YOUR NEXT YES

YES

End this study by writing a **one sentence summary** of what Jesus might be asking you to do in this next season. Write your sentence in the banner below as a symbol of saying "YES" to God.

LEADING MADE EASY

MEANT FOR GOOD
LEADER'S GUIDE

If you are reading this, you have likely agreed to lead a group through the *Meant for Good Study Guide*. Thank you! What you have chosen to do is important, and good fruit can come from studies like this. The rewards of being a leader are different from those of participating, and we hope you find your own walk with Jesus deepened by this experience. We hope that this *Leading Made Easy Leader's Guide* can help sharpen your skills and help you feel confident and prepared going into each group gathering.

The *Meant for Good Study Guide* is a 6-session study built around video content and small-group interaction.

As the group leader, your role is not to answer all the questions or reteach the content—the video, book, and study guide will do most of that work. Your job is to guide the experience.

BEFORE YOU BEGIN

Before your first meeting, make sure the participants have a copy of this study guide so they can follow along and have their answers written out ahead of time. Also have them go through the *What's This Study All About?* section at the beginning of the book ahead of your first group gathering. Alternatively, you can hand out the study guides at your first meeting and give the group members some time to look over the material and ask any preliminary questions.

Generally, the ideal size for a group is between eight to ten people, which ensures everyone will have enough time to participate in discussions. If you have more people, you might want to break up the main group into smaller subgroups after watching the video together. Encourage everyone to commit to attending the duration of the study, as this will help the group members get to know each other, create stability for the group, and help you know how to prepare each week.

Each of the sessions begins with *Gathering Transition Time* questions. These are designed to be answered in three words or less. Ideally, you want everyone in the group to get a chance to answer.

With the rest of the study, a free-flowing discussion is most effective. But with the opening *Transition Time* questions, you can go around the circle. Encourage shy people to share, but don't force them.

Study & Seek is the personal study component of the *Meant For Good Study Guide* containing Bible study and reflection materials for each session. *Study & Seek* is intended for individuals to do in between gatherings. Let your group members know about this *Study & Seek* section and encourage them to go at their own pace doing a little each day or all at once between group gatherings.

MATERIALS NEEDED FOR A SUCCESSFUL GATHERING

- *Meant for Good* DVD or steaming access
- A *Meant for Good Study Guide* for each group member
- Bible(s)
- Pen or pencil for each person

WEEKLY PREPARATION

As the leader, there are a few things you should do to prepare for each meeting:

- *Read through the session itself.* This will help you to become familiar with the content and know how to structure the discussion times.

- *Decide which questions you definitely want to go through.* Based on how much time you have, you may not be able to get through all of the discussion in each group gathering, so prioritize what feels the most important for your group.

- *Keep an eye on the time.*

- *Pray for your group.* Spend some time in prayer for your group members throughout the week and ask God to lead them as they study His Word.

- *Bring extra supplies to your meeting.* The members should bring their own pens for writing notes, but it's a good idea to have extras available for those who forget. They should also bring their *Meant for Good Study Guide* each week. You may also want to bring paper and additional Bibles.

Note that in many cases there will be no one "right" answer to the question. Answers will vary, especially when the group members are being asked to share their personal experiences.

Stay connected with the people in your group. During the first gathering you will want to find out the best way to individually reach out to each person. You'll then want to send encouragement throughout the week or follow up on what they shared in prior weeks in order to stay connected outside of your group time. As your people come to mind, reach out to them. Show them God's love, grace, and pursuit.

STRUCTURING THE GATHERING TIME

You will need to determine with your group how long you want to meet each week so you can plan your time accordingly. This study is set up to have gatherings last about 90 minutes. Though each week is a little different, the next page offers a suggested schedule for how to best use your time at each gathering. Note that you will not be able to use the maximum amount of time for each section. Decide beforehand what you want to take more and less time on as a group.

As the group leader, it is up to you to keep track of the time and keep things moving along according to your schedule. You might want to set a timer for each segment so both you and the group members know when your time is up.

(Note that there are some good phone apps for timers that play a gentle chime or other pleasant sounds instead of a disruptive noise.)

Don't be concerned if the group members are quiet or slow to share. People are often quiet when they are pulling together their ideas, and this might be a new experience for them. Just ask a question and let it hang in the air until someone shares. You can then say, "Thank you. What about others? What comes to mind for you?"

SUGGESTED GATHERING OUTLINE

▶ *GATHERING TRANSITION TIME (5-10 MINUTES)*

Before you dive in, take a few minutes to answer a question or two to prep your minds and hearts for the teaching.

▶ *HEAR FROM MEGAN—VIDEO (15-20 MINUTES)*

Each session is kicked off with a video teaching from Megan Fate Marshman.

▶ *THINK BEFORE YOU SPEAK (5 MINUTES)*

In this section you all will unpack a passage of scripture and short commentary on the topic Megan set up, all helping you better understand who God is.

▶ *GROUP DISCUSSION (30-40 MINUTES)*

In *Being Made Like Jesus*, you will lead a discussion through Scripture which ties into the session theme and is expressed through a visual chart or graphic.

▶ *RECEIVE BLESSING (5 MINUTES)*

Each week follower the prompt and offer a blessing over your group before you close in prayer. This is a vital practice that fills the heart and focuses the spirit.

▶ *CLOSING PRAYER (5 MINUTES)*

Encourage your group to engage the personal study material in between gatherings and be sure to track prayer requests as well as praises week to week.

GROUP DYNAMICS

Leading a group through the *Meant for Good Study Guide* will prove to be highly rewarding both to you and your group members. However, this doesn't mean you will not encounter any challenges along the way! Discussions can get off track. Group members may not be sensitive to the needs and ideas of others. Some might worry they will be expected to talk about matters that make them feel awkward. Others may express comments that result in disagreements. To help ease this strain on you and the group, consider the following ground rules:

When someone raises a question or comment that is off the main topic, suggest you deal with it another time, or, if you feel led to go in that direction, let the group know you will be spending some time discussing it.

If someone asks a question you don't know how to answer, admit it and move on. At your discretion, feel free to invite group members to comment on questions that call for personal experience.

If you find one or two people are dominating the discussion time, direct a few questions to others in the group. Outside the main group time, ask the more dominating members to help you draw out the quieter ones. Work to make them a part of the solution instead of the problem.

When a disagreement occurs, encourage the group members to process the matter in love. Encourage those on opposite sides to restate what they heard the other side say about the matter, and then invite each side to evaluate if that perception is accurate. Lead the group in examining other Scriptures related to the topic and look for common ground.

When any of these issues arise, encourage your group members to follow these words from the Bible: "Love one another" (John 13:34), "If it is possible, as far as it depends on you, live at peace with everyone" (Romans 12:18), and "Be quick to listen, slow to speak and slow to become angry" (James 1:19). This will make your group time more rewarding and beneficial for everyone who attends.

"ONE DOES NOT **SURRENDER** A LIFE IN AN INSTANT. THAT WHICH IS **LIFELONG** CAN ONLY BE SURRENDERED IN A LIFETIME."

—ELISABETH ELLIOT

BIBLIOGRAPHY

SESSION 1

Coe, John. "Spiritual Theology: A Theological-Experiential Methodology for Bridging the Sanctification Gap." *Journal of Spiritual Formation and Soul Care 2*, no. 1 (May 2009): 4–43. doi:10.1177/193979090900200102.

Lewis, C.S . *The C. S. Lewis Bible*, Grand Rapids, MI: HarperCollins. 2012.

Marshman, Megan Fate. *Meant for Good*. Grand Rapids, MI: Zondervan. 2020.

Schreiner, Thomas R. *Romans*. Grand Rapids, MI: Baker, 2018.

SESSION 2

Calcuta, Teresa de, and Jean Maalouf. *Mother Teresa: Essential Writings*. Maryknoll, NY: Orbis Books, 2003.

Marshman, Megan Fate. *Meant for Good*. Grand Rapids, MI: Zondervan. 2020.

Willard, Dallas. *Renovation of the Heart: Putting on the Character of Christ*. Colorado Springs, CO: NavPress, 2012.

Ten Boom, Corrie. "Corrie Ten Boom Quote." A. Accessed March 24, 2020. https://www.azquotes.com/quote/32077.

SESSION 3

Arthur, Kay. *How to Study Your Bible*. Eugene, OR: Harvest House, 2001.

Foster, Richard J. *Celebration of Discipline: The Path to Spiritual Growth*. San Francisco: HarperOne, 2018.

Marshman, Megan Fate. *Meant for Good*. Grand Rapids, MI: Zondervan Publishing. 2020.

"*Meno* Meaning in Bible—New Testament Greek Lexicon—King James Version." *Bible Study Tools*. Accessed March 25, 2020. https://www.biblestudytools.com/lexicons/greek/kjv/meno.html.

"The Book of Romans." BibleProject. Accessed March 27, 2020. https://bibleproject.com/explore/romans/.

"Henri J.M. Nouwen Quote" Quotefancy. Accessed March 27, 2020. https://quotefancy.com/quote/823457/Henri-J-M-Nouwen-Jesus-invites-us-to-abide-in-his-love-That-means-to-dwell-with-all-that.

SESSION 4

Arnold, Clinton E. *Zondervan Illustrated Bible Backgrounds Commentary*. Grand Rapids, MI: Zondervan, 2002.

Lawrence, and Joseph de. Beaufort. *Brother Lawrence: The Practice of the Presence of God*. Cincinnati, OH: Forward Movement Publications, n.d.

Marshman, Megan Fate. *Meant for Good*. Grand Rapids, MI: Zondervan, 2020.

TerKeurst, Lysa. Blog: "Why am I scared to pray boldly?" September 16, 2010. Accessed March 30, 2020. https://lysaterkeurst.com/2010/09/why-am-i-scared-to-pray-boldly/.

NIV, *Cultural Backgrounds Study Bible: Bringing to Life the Ancient World of Scripture.* Grand Rapids, MI, 2017.

SESSION 5

Barker, Kenneth L., and John R. Kohlenberger. *The Expositor's Bible Commentary: Abridged Edition.* Grand Rapids, MI: Zondervan, 1994.

Halley, Henry H. *Halley's Bible Handbook: An Abbreviated Bible Commentary: A General View of the Bible, Notes on Each of the Bible Books, Miscellaneous Bible Information, Notes on Obscure Passages, Related Historical Data.* Grason, MN: 1964.

King, Martin Luther Jr. "Loving Your Enemies." Sermon by Martin Luther King, Jr. at Dexter Avenue Baptist Church, Montgomery, Alabama, November 17, 1957.

Marshman, Megan Fate. *Meant for Good.* Grand Rapids, MI: Zondervan Publishing. 2020.

NIV, *Cultural Backgrounds Study Bible: Bringing to Life the Ancient World of Scripture.* Grand Rapids, MI, 2017.

"Prophecy Plants Hope and Salvation in the Book of Isaiah." BibleProject. Accessed April 1, 2020. https://bibleproject.com/explore/isaiah/.

Ten Boom, Corrie. *Tramp for the Lord.* Old Tappan, NJ: Revell, 1974.

Tozer, A.W. *Experiencing the Presence of God: Teachings from the Book of Hebrews.* Compiled and edited by James L. Snyder. Bloomington, MN: Bethany House, 2010.

SESSION 6

Elliot, Elisabeth. *Shadow of the Almighty: The Life & Testament of Jim Elliot.* San Francisco: Harper & Row, 2011.

Goff, Bob. *Love Does.* Nashville, TN: Thomas Nelson, 2014.

Marshman, Megan Fate. *Meant for Good.* Grand Rapids, MI: Zondervan Publishing. 2020.

Willard, Dallas. *Living in Christ's Presence: Final Words on Heaven and the Kingdom of God.* Chicago IL: InterVarsity Press, 2017.

MEANT FOR GOOD

THE **ADVENTURE** OF TRUSTING GOD AND HIS PLANS FOR YOU

Megan Fate Marshman

Meant for Good is a power-packed, biblical look at the truth that you really can trust God's plan for your life—no matter what your life looks like right now. Dynamic Bible teacher Megan Fate Marshman will help you discover how to stop discounting yourself from a hopeful future, start living in active dependence on God, and find your way to the good plan He has for you.

With authenticity and revelatory insights into the character of God, Megan shares an engaging and fresh look at the core themes within the well-loved scripture of Jeremiah 29:11-14. Through winsome and inspiring stories, *Meant for Good* will show you how to trust God in your daily life and, more importantly, how to trust God's definition of good above your own.

You will discover:
- That your not-enoughness is exactly enough for God, and that in fact, you have everything you need to take that first step into the life God has for you.
- How to stop counting yourself out, because Jesus never has. God is up to something really good, and He's inviting you to join Him.
- How to hear and respond to God's voice, and intentionally grow a personal, intimate relationship with Him.
- How to defeat anxiety, trust God with all you're carrying and worrying about, and experience a life of freedom in relying on God daily.

God has a good plan for you—a plan to give you a hope and a future.

Are you ready to believe it?

Available in stores and online!

BIBLE STUDY SOURCE
for women
powered by ChurchSource

Connecting you with the best in

BIBLE STUDY RESOURCES

from many of the world's

MOST TRUSTED BIBLE TEACHERS

MEGAN MARSHMAN   **JENNIE ALLEN**   **JADA EDWARDS**   **LISA WHITTLE**

Providing

WOMEN'S MINISTRY AND SMALL GROUP LEADERS

with the **INSPIRATION, ENCOURAGEMENT, AND RESOURCES** to grow your ministry

powered by ChurchSource

FIND THE *perfect* BIBLE STUDY
for you and your group in 5 MINUTES *or* LESS!

*Find the right study for your women's group
by answering four easy questions:*

1. WHAT TYPE OF STUDY DO YOU WANT TO DO?

- *Book of the Bible:* Dive deep into the study of a Bible character, or go through a complete book of the Bible systematically, or add tools to your Bible study methods toolkit.

- *Topical Issues:* Have a need in a specific area of life? Study the Scriptures that pertain to that need. Topics include prayer, joy, purpose, balance, identity in Christ, and more.

2. WHAT LEVEL OF TIME COMMITMENT BETWEEN SESSIONS WOULD YOU LIKE?

- *None:* No personal homework
- *Minimal:* Less than 30 minutes of homework
- *Moderate:* 30 minutes to one hour of homework
- *Substantial:* An hour or more of homework

3. WHAT IS YOUR GROUP'S BIBLE KNOWLEDGE?

- *Beginner:* Group is comprised mostly of women who are new to the Bible or who don't feel confident in their Bible knowledge.

- *Intermediate:* Group has some experience with studying the Bible, and they have some familiarity with the stories in the Bible.

- *Advanced:* Group is comfortable with the Bible, and can handle the challenge of searching the Scriptures for themselves.

4. WHAT FORMAT DO YOU PREFER?

- *Print and Video:* Watch a Bible teacher on video, followed by a facilitated discussion.
- *Print Only:* Have the group leader give a short talk and lead a discussion of a study guide or a book.

Get Started! Plug your answers into the **Bible Study Finder**, and discover the studies that best fit your group!

Check out the Bible Study Finder at:
BibleStudySourcForWomen.com

NOTES

NOTES